Books by Anthony Hecht

MILLIONS OF STRANGE SHADOWS (1977)
THE HARD HOURS (1967)
A SUMMONING OF STONES (1954)

Translation

AESCHYLUS' SEVEN AGAINST THEBES (1973)
(*with Helen Bacon*)

MILLIONS OF STRANGE SHADOWS

"MILLIONS OF STRANGE SHADOWS "

POEMS BY

ANTHONY HECHT

Atheneum   New York   1980

ACKNOWLEDGMENT TO George Dimock, Jr. and William Arrowsmith for assistance in translating the chorus from Sophocles' *Oedipus at Kolonos*.

Green: An Epistle was the Phi Beta Kappa poem for Swarthmore in 1971; *The Odds* was the Phi Beta Kappa poem for Harvard, 1975.

THE TRANSLATION OF Voltaire's *Poem Upon the Lisbon Disaster* originally appeared in a limited edition published by *The Penmaen Press*.

THE FOLLOWING POEMS originally appeared in *The New Yorker*: Green: An Epistle; Peripeteia; After the Rain; The Odds; The Lull; Fifth Avenue Parade.

OTHER POEMS appeared as follows: The Cost (*Encounter*); Black Boy in the Dark, An Autumnal (*Harpers*); Dichtung und Wahrheit (*The American Scholar*); A Voice at a Seance (*Antaeus*); Somebody's Life (*Hudson Review*); A Lot of Night Music (*Ploughshares*); Swan Dive; The Feast of Stephen (*Georgia Review*); "Auguries of Innocence" (*Harvard Advocate*); Apples for Paul Suttman (*Wild Places*); The Hunt (*New Statesman*); Exile; Coming Home (*Times Literary Supplement*); The Ghost in the Martini (*New American Review*); Going the Rounds (*Quarterly Review of Literature*).

Library of Congress Cataloging in Publication Data

Hecht, Anthony, 1923—
    Millions of strange shadows.

    I. Title.
PS 3358.E28M5   1977   811'.5'4   76—48223
ISBN 0–689–10784–6 (clothbound)
ISBN 0–689–11116–9 (paperback)

For HELEN

> *of whom I have*
> *Receiv'd a second life . . .*

CONTENTS

THE COST   *3*

BLACK BOY IN THE DARK   *6*

AN AUTUMNAL   *8*

"DICHTUNG UND WAHRHEIT"   *9*

A VOICE AT A SEANCE   *12*

GREEN: AN EPISTLE   *13*

SOMEBODY'S LIFE   *18*

A LOT OF NIGHT MUSIC   *19*

A BIRTHDAY POEM   *21*

RETREAT   *24*

COMING HOME   *25*

PRAISE FOR KOLONOS   *28*

SESTINA D'INVERNO   *30*

ROME   *32*

SWAN DIVE   *33*

"AUGURIES OF INNOCENCE"   *35*

PERIPETEIA   *36*

AFTER THE RAIN   *39*

APPLES FOR PAUL SUTTMAN   *41*

THE HUNT   *43*

EXILE   *45*

THE FEAST OF STEPHEN   *46*

THE ODDS   *48*

APPREHENSIONS   *50*

THE GHOST IN THE MARTINI   *56*

GOING THE ROUNDS   *60*

GOLIARDIC SONG   *63*

"GLADNESS OF THE BEST"   *64*

POEM UPON THE LISBON DISASTER   *66*

FIFTH AVENUE PARADE   *73*

THE LULL   *74*

MILLIONS OF STRANGE SHADOWS

THE COST

Why, let the stricken deer go weep,
The hart ungallèd play . . .

Think how some excellent, lean torso hugs
    The brink of weight and speed,
Coasting the margins of those rival tugs
    Down the thin path of friction,
The athlete's dancing vectors, the spirit's need,
    And muscle's cleanly diction,

Clean as a Calder, whose interlacing ribs
    Depend on one another,
Or a keen heeling of tackle, fluttering jibs
    And slotted centerboards,
A fleet of breasting gulls riding the smother
    And puzzle of heaven's wards.

Instinct with joy, a young Italian banks
    Smoothly around the base
Of Trajan's column, feeling between his flanks
    That cool, efficient beast,
His Vespa, at one with him in a centaur's race,
    Fresh from a Lapith feast,

And his Lapith girl behind him. Both of them lean
    With easy nonchalance
Over samphire-tufted cliffs which, though unseen,
    Are known, as the body knows
New risks and tilts, terrors and loves and wants,
    Deeply inside its clothes.

She grips the animal-shouldered naked skin
    Of his fitted leather jacket,
Letting a wake of hair float out of the spin
    And dazzled rinse of air,
Yet for all their headlong lurch and flatulent racket
    They seem to loiter there,

Forever aslant in their moment and the mind's eye.
    Meanwhile, around the column
There also turn, and turn eternally,
    Two thousand raw recruits
And scarred veterans coiling the stone in solemn
    Military pursuits,

The heft and grit of the emperor's Dacian Wars
    That lasted fifteen years.
All of that youth and purpose is, of course,
    No more than so much dust.
And even Trajan, of his imperial peers
    Accounted "the most just,"

Honored by Dante, by Gregory the Great
    Saved from eternal Hell,
Swirls in the motes kicked up by the cough and spate
    Of the Vespa's blue exhaust,
And a voice whispers inwardly, "My soul,
    It is the cost, the cost,"

Like some unhinged Othello, who's just found out
    That justice is no more,
While Cassio, Desdemona, Iago shout
    Like true Venetians all,
"Go screw yourself; all's fair in love and war!"
    And the bright standards fall.

Better they should not hear that whispered phrase,
    The young Italian couple;
Surely the mind in all its brave assays
    Must put much thinking by,
To be, as Yeats would have it, free and supple
    As a long-legged fly.

Look at their slender purchase, how they list
    Like a blown clipper, brought
To the lively edge of peril, to the kissed
    Lip, the victor's crown,
The prize of life. Yet one unbodied thought
    Could topple them, bring down

The whole shebang. And why should they take thought
    Of all that ancient pain,
The Danube winters, the nameless young who fought,
    The blood's uncertain lease?
Or remember that that fifteen-year campaign
    Won seven years of peace?

BLACK BOY IN THE DARK

for Thomas Cornell

Peace, tawny slave, half me and half thy dam!
Did not thy hue bewray whose brat thou art,
. . .
Villain, thou mightst have been an emperor.

Summer. A hot, moth-populated night.
Yesterday's maples in the village park
Are boxed away into the vaults of dark,
To be returned tomorrow, like our flag,
Which was brought down from its post office height
At sunset, folded, and dumped in a mailbag.

Wisdom, our Roman matron, perched on her throne
In front of the library, the Civil War
Memorial (History and Hope) no more
Are braced, trustworthy figures. Some witching skill
Softly dismantled them, stone by heavy stone,
And the small town, like Bethlehem, lies still.

And it is still at the all-night service station,
Where Andy Warhol's primary colors shine
In simple commercial glory, the Esso sign
Revolving like a funland lighthouse, where
An eighteen-year-old black boy clocks the nation,
Reading a comic book in a busted chair.

Our solitary guardian of the law
Of diminishing returns? The President,
Addressing the first contingent of draftees sent
To Viet Nam, was brief: "Life is not fair,"
He said, and was right, of course. Everyone saw
What happened to him in Dallas. We were there,

We suffered, we were Whitman. And now the boy
Daydreams about the White House, the rising shares
Of Standard Oil, the whited sepulchres.
But what, after all, has he to complain about,
This expendable St. Michael we employ
To stay awake and keep the darkness out?

AN AUTUMNAL

The lichens, like a gorgeous, soft disease
        In rust and gold rosette
Emboss the bouldered wall, and creepers seize
        In their cup-footed fret,

Ravelled and bare, such purchase as affords.
        The sap-tide slides to ebb,
And leafstems, like the drumsticks of small birds,
        Lie snagged in a spiderweb.

Down at the stonework base, among the stump-
        Fungus and feather moss,
Dead leaves are sunken in a shallow sump
        Of energy and loss,

Enriched now with the colors of old coins
        And brilliance of wet leather.
An earthen tea distills at the roots-groins
        Into the smoky weather

A deep, familiar essence of the year:
        A sweet fetor, a ghost
Of foison, gently welcoming us near
        To humus, mulch, compost.

The last mosquitoes lazily hum and play
        Above the yeasting earth
A feeble *Gloria* to this cool decay
        Or casual dirge of birth.

"DICHTUNG UND WAHRHEIT"

for Cyrus Hoy

I

The Discus Thrower's marble heave,
    Captured in mid-career,
That polished poise, that Parian arm
    Sleeved only in the air,
Vesalian musculature, white
    As the mid-winter moon—
This, and the clumsy snapshot of
    An infantry platoon,
Those grubby and indifferent men,
    Lounging in bivouac,
Their rifles aimless in their laps,
    Stop history in its tracks.

We who are all aswim in time,
    We, "the inconstant ones,"
How can such fixture speak to us?
    The chisel and the lens
Deal in a taxidermy
    Of our arrested flights,
And by their brute translation we
    Turn into Benthamites.
Those soldiers, like some senior class,
    Were they prepared to dye
In silver nitrate images
    Behind the camera's eye?

It needs a Faust to animate
    The wan homunculus,
Construe the stark, unchanging text,
    Winkle the likes of us
Out of a bleak geology
    That art has put to rest,
And by a sacred discipline

Give breath back to the past.
How, for example, shall I read
The expression on my face
Among that company of men
In that unlikely place?

I I

Easy enough to claim, in the dawn of hindsight,
That Mozart's music perfectly enacts
Pastries and powdered wigs, an architecture
Of white and gold rosettes, balanced parterres.
More difficult to know how the spirit learns
Its scales, or the exact dimensions of fear:
The nameless man dressed head-to-foot in black,
Come to commission a requiem in a hurry.
In the diatonic house there are many mansions:
A hunting lodge in the mountains, a peaceable
      cloister,
A first-class restaurant near the railroad yards,
But also a seedy alms-house, the granite prisons
And oubliettes of the soul. Just how such truth
Gets itself stated in pralltrillers and mordents
Not everyone can say. But the 'cellist,
Leaning over his labors, his eyes closed,
Is engaged in that study, blocking out, for the
      moment,
Audience, hall, and a great part of himself
In what, not wrongly, might be called research,
Or the most private kind of honesty.

We begin with the supreme donnée, the world,
Upon which every text is commentary,
And yet they play each other, the oak-leaf cured
In sodden ditches of autumn darkly confirms

Our words; and by the frailest trifles
(A doubt, a whisper, and a handkerchief)
Venetian pearl and onyx are cast away.
It is, in the end, the solitary scholar
Who returns us to the freshness of the text,
Which returns to us the freshness of the world
In which we find ourselves, like replicas,
Dazzled by glittering dawns, upon a stage.
Pentelic balconies give on the east;
The clouds are scrolled, bellied in apricot,
Adrift in pools of Scandinavian blue.
Light crisps the terraces of dolomite.
Enter The Prologue, who at once declares,
"We begin with the supreme donnée, the word."

A VOICE AT A SEANCE

It is rather strange to be speaking, but I know you are
    there
Wanting to know, as if it were worth knowing.
Nor is it important that I died in combat
In a good cause or an indifferent one.
Such things, it may surprise you, are not regarded.
Something too much of this.

You are bound to be disappointed,
Wanting to know, are there any trees?
It is all different from what you suppose,
And the darkness is not darkness exactly,
But patience, silence, withdrawal, the sad knowledge
That it was almost impossible not to hurt anyone
Whether by action or inaction.
At the beginning of course there was a sense of loss,
Not of one's own life, but of what seemed
The easy, desirable lives one might have led.
Fame or wealth are hard to achieve,
And goodness even harder;
But the cost of all of them is a familiar deformity
Such as everyone suffers from:
An allergy to certain foods, nausea at the sight of blood,
A slight impediment of speech, shame at one's own body,
A fear of heights or claustrophobia.
What you learn has nothing whatever to do with joy,
Nor with sadness, either. You are mostly silent.
You come to a gentle indifference about being thought
Either a fool or someone with valuable secrets.
It may be that the ultimate wisdom
Lies in saying nothing.
I think I may already have said too much.

GREEN: AN EPISTLE

This urge, wrestle, resurrection of dry sticks,
Cut stems struggling to put down feet,
What saint strained so much,
Rose on such lopped limbs to a new life?
                                    THEODORE ROETHKE

I write at last of the one forbidden topic
We, by a truce, have never touched upon:
Resentment, malice, hatred so inwrought
With moral inhibitions, so at odds with
The home-movie of yourself as patience, kindness,
And Charlton Heston playing Socrates,
That almost all of us were taken in,
Yourself not least, as to a giant Roxy,
Where the lights dimmed and the famous allegory
Of Good and Evil, clearly identified
By the unshaven surliness of the Bad Guys,
The virginal meekness of the ingénue,
Seduced us straight into that perfect world
Of Justice under God. Art for the sake
Of money, glamour, ego, self-deceit.
When we emerged into the assaulting sunlight,
We had a yen, like bad philosophers,
To go back to stay forever, there in the dark
With the trumpets, horses, and ancient Certitudes
On which, as we know, this great nation was founded,
Washington crossed the Delaware, and so forth.
And all of us, for an hour or so after,
Were Humphrey Bogart dating Ingrid Bergman,
Walking together but incommunicado
Till subway and homework knocked us out of it.
Yet even then, whatever we returned to
Was not, although we thought it was, the world.

I write at last on this topic because I am safe
Here in this grubby little border town
With its one cheap hotel. No one has my address.

The food is bad, the wine is too expensive,
And the local cathedral marred by restorations.
But from my balcony I view the east
For miles and, if I lean, the local sunsets
That bathe a marble duke with what must be
Surely the saddest light I have ever seen.
The air is thin and cool at this elevation,
And my desk wobbles unless propped with
    matchbooks.

It began, I suppose, as a color, yellow-green,
The tincture of spring willows, not so much color
As the sensation of color, haze that took shape
As a light scum, a doily of minutiae
On the smooth pool and surface of your mind.
A founding colony, Pilgrim amoebas
Descended from the gaseous flux when Zeus
Tossed down his great original thunderbolt
That flashed in darkness like an electric tree
Or the lit-up veins in an old arthritic hand.

Here is the microscope one had as a child,
The Christmas gift of some forgotten uncle.
Here is the slide with a drop of cider vinegar
As clear as gin, clear as your early mind.
Look down, being most careful not to see
Your own eye in the mirror underneath,
Which will appear, unless your view is right,
As a darkness on the face of the first waters.
When all is silvery and brilliant, look:
The long, thin, darting shapes, the flagellates,
Rat-tailed, ambitious, lash themselves along—
Those humble, floating ones, those simple cells
Content to be borne on whatever tide,
Trustful, the very image of consent—
These are the frail, unlikely origins,
Scarcely perceived, of all you shall become.
Scarcely perceived? But at this early age

(What are you, one or two?) you have no
    knowledge,
Nor do your folks, nor could the gravest doctors
Suspect that anything was really wrong.
Nor see the pale beginnings, lace endeavors
That with advancing ages shall mature
Into sea lettuce, beard the rocky shore
With a light green of soft and tidal hair.

      Whole eras, seemingly without event,
Now scud the glassy pool processionally
Until one day, misty, uncalendared,
As mild and unemphatic as a schwa,
Vascular tissue, conduit filaments
Learn how to feed the outposts of that small
Emerald principate. Now there are roots,
The filmy gills of toadstools, crested fern,
Quillworts, and foxtail mosses, and at last
Snapweed, loment, trillium, grass, herb Robert.
How soundlessly, shyly this came about,
One thinks today. But that is not the truth.
It was, from the first, an everlasting war
Conducted, as always, at gigantic cost.
Think of the droughts, the shifts of wind and
    weather,
The many seeds washed to some salt conclusion
Or brought to rest at last on barren ground.
Think of some inching tendrils worming down
In hope of water, blind and white as death.
Think of the strange mutations life requires.
Only the toughest endured, themselves much
    altered,
Trained in the cripple's careful sciences
Of mute accommodation. The survivors
Were all, one way or another, amputees
Who learned to live with their stumps, like
    Brueghel's beggars.

Yet, for all that, it clearly was a triumph,
Considering, as one must, what was to come.
And, even by themselves, those fields of clover,
Cattails, marsh bracken, water-lily pads
Stirred by the lightest airs, pliant, submissive—
Who could have called their slow creation *rage*?

Consider, as one must, what was to come.
Great towering conifers, deciduous,
Rib-vaulted elms, the banyan, oak, and palm,
Sequoia forests of vindictiveness
That also would go down on the death list
And, buried deep beneath alluvial shifts,
Would slowly darken into lakes of coal
And then under exquisite pressure turn
Into tiny diamonds of pure hate.
The delicate fingers of the clematis
Feeling their way along a face of shale
With all the ingenuity of spite.
The indigestible thistle of revenge.
And your most late accomplishment, the rose.
Until at last, what we might designate
As your Third Day, behold a world of green:
Color of hope, of the Church's springtide
        vestments,
The primal wash, heraldic hue of envy.
But in what pre-lapsarian disguise!
Strangers and those who do not know you well
(Yourself not least) are quickly taken in
By a summery prospect, shades of innocence.
Like that young girl, a sort of chance
        acquaintance,
Seven or eight she was, on the New York
        Central,
Who, with a blue-eyed, beatific smile,
Shouted with joy, "Look, Mommy, quick. Look.
        Daisies!"

These days, with most of us at a safe distance,
You scarcely know yourself. Whole weeks go by
Without your remembering that enormous effort,
Ages of disappointment, the long ache
Of motives twisted out of recognition,
The doubt and hesitation all submerged
In those first clear waters, that untroubled pool.
Who could have hoped for this eventual peace?
Moreover, there are moments almost of bliss,
A sort of recompense, in which your mood
Sorts with the peach endowments of late sunlight
On a snowfield or on the breaker's froth
Or the white steeple of the local church.
Or, like a sunbather, whose lids retain
A greenish, gemmed impression of the sun
In lively, fluctuant geometries,
You sometimes contemplate a single image,
Utterly silent, utterly at rest.
It is of someone, a stranger, quite unknown,
Sitting alone in a foreign-looking room,
Gravely intent at a table propped with match-
        books,
Writing this very poem—about me.

SOMEBODY'S LIFE

I

Cliff-high, sunlit, in the tawny warmth of youth,
He gazed down at the breakneck rocks below,
Entranced by the water's loose attacks of jade,
The sousing waves, the interminable, blind
Fury of scattered opals, flung tiaras,
Full, hoisted, momentary chandeliers.
He spent most of the morning there alone.
He smoked, recalled some lines of poetry,
Felt himself claimed by such rash opulence:
These were the lofty figures of his soul.
What was it moved him in all that swash and
        polish?
Against an imperial sky of lupine blue,
Suspended, as it seemed to him, forever,
Blazed a sun-flooded gem of the first water.

II

Blazed, as it seemed, forever. Was this the secret
Gaudery of self-love, or a blood-bidden,
Involuntary homage to the world?
As it happens, he was doomed never to know.
At times in darkened rooms he thought he heard
The soft ruckus of patiently torn paper,
The sea's own noise, the elderly slop and suck
Of hopeless glottals. Once, in a bad dream,
He saw himself stranded on the wet flats,
As limp as kelp, among putrescent crabs.
But to the very finish he remembered
The flash and force, the crests, the heraldry,
Those casual epergnes towering up
Like Easter trinkets of the tzarevitch.

A LOT OF NIGHT MUSIC

Even a Pyrrhonist
Who knows only that he can never know
        (But adores a paradox)
Would admit it's getting dark. Pale as a wrist-
        Watch numeral glow,
Fireflies build a sky among the phlox,

        Imparting their faint light
Conservatively only to themselves.
        Earthmurk and flowerscent
Sweeten the homes of ants. Comes on the night
        When the mind rockets and delves
In blind hyperbolas of its own bent.

        Above, the moon at large,
Muse-goddess, slightly polluted by the runs
        Of American astronauts,
(Poor, poxed Diana, laid open to the charge
        Of social Actaeons)
Mildly solicits our petty cash and thoughts.

        At once with their votive mites,
Out of the woods and woodwork poets come,
        Hauling their truths and booty,
Each one a Phosphor, writing by his own lights,
        And with a diesel hum
Of mosquitoes or priests, proffer their wordy
        duty.

        They speak in tongues, no doubt;
High glossolalia, runic gibberish.
        Some are like desert saints,
Wheat-germ ascetics, draped in pelt and clout.
        Some come in schools, like fish.
These make their litany of dark complaints;

Those laugh and rejoice
At liberation from the bonds of gender,
Race, morals and mind,
As well as meter, rhyme and the human voice.
Still others strive to render
The cross-word world in perfectly declined

Pronouns, starting with ME.
Yet there are honest voices to be heard:
The crickets keep their vigil
Among the grass; in some invisible tree
Anonymously a bird
Whistles a fioritura, a light, vestigial

Reminder of a time,
An Aesopic Age when all the beasts were moral
And taught their ways to men;
Some herbal dream, some chlorophyll sublime
In which Apollo's laurel
Blooms in a world made innocent again.

A BIRTHDAY POEM

June 22, 1976

Like a small cloud, like a little hovering ghost
      Without substance or edges,
Like a crowd of numbered dots in a sick child's puzzle,
    A loose community of midges
Sways in the carven shafts of noon that coast
Down through the summer trees in a golden dazzle.

Intent upon such tiny copter flights,
      The eye adjusts its focus
To those billowings about ten feet away,
    That hazy, woven hocus-pocus
Or shell game of the air, whose casual sleights
Leave us unable certainly to say

What lies behind it, or what sets it off
      With fine diminishings,
Like the pale towns Mantegna chose to place
    Beyond the thieves and King of Kings:
Those domes, theatres and temples, clear enough
On that mid-afternoon of our disgrace.

And we know at once it would take an act of will
      Plus a firm, inquiring squint
To ignore those drunken motes and concentrate
    On the blurred, unfathomed background tint
Of deep sea-green Holbein employed to fill
The space behind his ministers of state,

As if one range slyly obscured the other.
      As, in the main, it does.
All of our Flemish distances disclose
    A clarity that never was:
Dwarf pilgrims in the green faubourgs of Mother
And Son, stunted cathedrals, shrunken cows.

It's the same with Time. Looked at *sub specie*
        Aeternitatis, from
The snow-line of some Ararat of years,
      Scholars remark those kingdoms come
To nothing, to grief, without the least display
Of anything so underbred as tears,

And with their Zeiss binoculars descry
        Verduns and Waterloos,
The man-made mushroom's deathly overplus,
      Caesars and heretics and Jews
Gone down in blood, without batting an eye,
As if all history were deciduous.

It's when we come to shift the gears of tense
        That suddenly we note
A curious excitement of the heart
      And slight catch in the throat:—
When, for example, from the confluence
That bears all things away I set apart

The inexpressible lineaments of your face,
        Both as I know it now,
By heart, by sight, by reverent touch and study,
      And as it once was years ago,
Back in some inaccessible time and place,
Fixed in the vanished camera of somebody.

You are four years old here in this photograph.
        You are turned out in style,
In a pair of bright red sneakers, a birthday gift.
      You are looking down at them with a smile
Of pride and admiration, half
Wonder and half joy, at the right and the left.

The picture is black and white, mere light and shade.
　　　　Even the sneakers' red
Has washed away in acids. A voice is spent,
　　　　Echoing down the ages in my head:
What is your substance, whereof are you made,
That millions of strange shadows on you tend?

O my most dear, I know the live imprint
　　　　Of that smile of gratitude,
Know it more perfectly than any book.
　　　　It brims upon the world, a mood
Of love, a mode of gladness without stint.
O that I may be worthy of that look.

RETREAT

Day peters out. Darkness wells up
　　From wheelrut, culvert, vacant drain;
But still a rooster glints with life,
　　High on a church's weather-vane;
The sun flings Mycenaean gold
　　Against a neighbor's window-pane.

COMING HOME

From the journals of John Clare

July 18, 1841

They take away our belts so that we must hold
Our trousers up. The truly mad don't bother
And thus are oddly hobbled. Also our laces
So that our shoes do flop about our feet.
But I'm permitted exercise abroad
And feeling rather down and melancholy
Went for a forest walk. There I met gypsies
And sought their help to make good my escape
From the mad house. I confessed I had no money
But promised I should furnish them fifty pounds.
We fixed on Saturday. But when I returned
They had disappeared in their Egyptian way.
The sun set up its starlight in the trees
Which the breeze made to twinkle. They left behind
An old wide awake hat on which I battened
As it might advantage me some later time.

July 20

Calmly, as though I purposed to converse
With the birds, as I am sometimes known to do,
I walked down the lane gently and was soon
In Enfield Town and then on the great York Road
Where it was all plain sailing, where no enemy
Displayed himself and I was without fear.
I made good progress, and by the dark of night
Skirted a marsh or pond and found a hovel
Floored with thick bales of clover and laid me down
As on the harvest of a summer field,
Companion to imaginary bees.
But I was troubled by uneasy dreams.
I thought my first wife lay in my left arm

And then somebody took her from my side
Which made me wake to hear someone say, "Mary,"
But nobody was by. I was alone.

* * *

I've made some progress, but being without food,
It is slower now, and I must void my shoes
Of pebbles fairly often, and rest myself.
I lay in a ditch to be out of the wind's way,
Fell into sleep for half an hour or so
And waked to find the left side of me soaked
With a foul scum and a soft mantling green.

* * *

I travel much at night, and I remember
Walking some miles under a brilliant sky
Almost dove-grey from closely hidden moonlight
Cast on the moisture of the atmosphere
Against which the tall trees on either side
Were unimaginably black and flat
And the puddles of the road flagstones of silver.

* * *

On the third day, stupid with weariness
And hunger, I assuaged my appetite
With eating grass, which seemed to taste like bread,
And seemed to do me good; and once, indeed,
It satisfied a king of Babylon.
I remember passing through the town of Buckden
And must have passed others as in a trance
For I recall none till I came to Stilton
Where my poor feet gave out. I found a tussock
Where I might rest myself, and as I lay down
I heard the voice of a young woman say,

"Poor creature," and another, older voice,
"He shams," but when I rose the latter said,
"O no he don't," as I limped quickly off.
I never saw those women, never looked back.

July 23

I was overtaken by a man and woman
Traveling by cart, and found them to be neighbors
From Helpstone where I used to live. They saw
My ragged state and gave me alms of fivepence
By which at the public house beside the bridge
I got some bread and cheese and two half-pints
And so was much refreshed, though scarcely able
To walk, my feet being now exceeding crippled
And I required to halt more frequently,
But greatly cheered at being in home's way.
I recognized the road to Peterborough
And all my hopes were up when there came towards
      me
A cart with a man, a woman and a boy.
When they were close, the woman leaped to the
      ground,
Seized both my hands and urged me towards the cart
But I refused and thought her either drunk
Or mad, but when I was told that she was Patty,
My second wife, I suffered myself to climb
Aboard and soon arrived at Northborough.
But Mary was not there. Neither could I discover
Anything of her more than the old story
That she was six years dead, intelligence
Of a doubtful newspaper some twelve years old;
But I would not be taken in by blarney
Having seen her very self with my two eyes
About twelve months ago, alive and young
And fresh and well and beautiful as ever.

27

PRAISE FOR KOLONOS

Come, let us praise this haven of strong horses,
unmatched, brilliant Kolonos, white with sunlight,
where the shy one, the nightingale, at evening
      flutes in the darkness,

the ivy dark, so woven of fruit and vine-leaves
no winter storms nor light of day can enter
this sanctuary of the dancing revels
      of Dionysos.

Here, under heaven's dew, blooms the narcissus,
crown of life's mother and her buried daughter,
of Earth and the Dark below; here, too, the sunburst
      flares of the crocus.

The river's ample springs, cool and unfailing,
rove and caress this green, fair-breasted landscape.
Here have the Muses visited with dances,
      and Aphrodite

has reined her chariot here. And here is something
unheard of in the fabulous land of Asia,
unknown to Doric earth—a thing immortal;
      gift of a goddess,

beyond the control of hands, tough, self-renewing,
an enduring wealth, passing through generations,
here only: the invincible grey-leafed olive.
      Agèd survivor

of all vicissitudes, it knows protection
of the All-Seeing Eye of Zeus, whose sunlight
always regards it, and of Grey-Eyed Athena.
      I have another

tribute of praise for this city, our mother:
the greatest gift of a god, a strength of horses,
strength of young horses, a power of the ocean,
      strength and a power.

O Lord Poseidon, you have doubly blessed us
with healing skills, on these roads first bestowing
the bit that gentles horses, the controlling
      curb and the bridle,

and the carved, feathering oar that skims and dances
like the white nymphs of water, conferring mastery
of ocean roads, among the spume and wind-blown
      prancing of stallions.

From SOPHOCLES' *Oedipus at Kolonos*

SESTINA D'INVERNO

Here in this bleak city of Rochester,
Where there are twenty-seven words for "snow,"
Not all of them polite, the wayward mind
Basks in some Yucatan of its own making,
Some coppery, sleek lagoon, or cinnamon island
Alive with lemon tints and burnished natives,

And O that we were there. But here the natives
Of this grey, sunless city of Rochester
Have sown whole mines of salt about their land
(Bare ruined Carthage that it is) while snow
Comes down as if The Flood were in the making.
Yet on that ocean Marvell called the mind

An ark sets forth which is itself the mind,
Bound for some pungent green, some shore whose
        natives
Blend coriander, cayenne, mint in making
Roasts that would gladden the Earl of Rochester
With sinfulness, and melt a polar snow.
It might be well to remember that an island

Was a blessed haven once, more than an island,
The grand, utopian dream of a noble mind.
In that kind climate the mere thought of snow
Was but a wedding cake; the youthful natives,
Unable to conceive of Rochester,
Made love, and were acrobatic in the making.

Dream as we may, there is far more to making
Do than some wistful reverie of an island,
Especially now when hope lies with the Rochester
Gas and Electric Co., which doesn't mind
Such profitable weather, while the natives
Sink, like Pompeians, under a world of snow.

The one thing indisputable here is snow,
The single verity of heaven's making,
Deeply indifferent to the dreams of the natives
And the torn hoarding-posters of some island.
Under our igloo skies the frozen mind
Holds to one truth: it is grey, and called Rochester.

No island fantasy survives Rochester,
Where to the natives destiny is snow
That is neither to our mind nor of our making.

ROME

Just as foretold, it all was there.
Bone china columns gently fluted
Among the cypress groves, and the reputed
Clarity of the air,

There was the sun-bleached skeleton
Of History with all its sins
Withered away, the slaves and citizens
Mercifully undone.

With here and there an armature
Of iron or a wall of brick,
It lay in unhistoric peace, a trick
Of that contrived, secure,

Arrested pterodactyl flight
Inside the museum's tank of glass;
And somehow quite unlike our Latin class
Sepias of the site,

Discoursed upon by Mr. Fish
In the familiar, rumpled suit,
Who tried to teach us the Ablative Absolute
And got part of his wish,

But a small part, and never traveled
On anything but the B. M. T.
Until the day of his death, when he would be,
At length, utterly graveled.

SWAN DIVE

Over a crisp regatta of lights, or a school
Of bobbling spoons, ovals of polished black
Kiss, link, and part, wriggle and ride in place
On the lilt and rippling slide of the waterback,
And glints go skittering in a down-wind race
On smooth librations of the swimming pool,

While overhead on the tensile jut and spring
Of the highest board, a saffroned diver toes
The sisal edge, rehearsing throughout his limbs
The flight of himself, from the arching glee to the
    close
Of wet, complete acceptance, when the world dims
To nothing at all in the ear's uproar and ring.

He backs away, and then, with a loping run
And leap of released ambition, lifts to a splendid
Realm of his own, a destined place in the air,
Where, in a wash of light, he floats suspended
Above the turquoise waters, the ravelled snare
Of snaking gold, the fractured, drunken sun,

And the squints of the foreshortened girls and boys
Below in a world of envies and desires,
Eying him rise on fonts of air to sheer
And shapely grace. His dream of himself requires
A flexed attention, emptiness, a clear
Uncumbered space and sleek Daedalian poise,

From which he bows his head with abrupt assent
And sails to a perfect sacrifice below—
To a scatter of flagstone shadows, a garbled flight
Of quavering anthelions, a slow
Tumult of haloes in green, cathedral light.
Behind him trails a bright dishevelment

Of rising carbuncles of air; he sees
Light spill across the undulant mercury film
Beyond which lies his breath. And now with a
    flutter
Of fountaining arms and into a final calm
He surfaces, clutching at the tiled gutter,
Where he rides limp and smilingly at ease.

But hoisting himself out, his weight returns
To normal, like sudden aging or weariness.
Tonight, full-length on a rumpled bed, alone,
He will redream it all: bathed in success
And sweat, he will achieve the chiselled stone
Of catatonia, for which his body yearns.

"AUGURIES OF INNOCENCE"

A small, unsmiling child,
Held upon her shoulder,
Stares from a photograph
Slightly out of kilter.
It slipped from a loaded folder
Where the income tax was filed.
The light seems cut in half
By a glum, October filter.

Of course, the child is right.
The unleafed branches knot
Into hopeless riddles behind him
And the air is clearly cold.
Given the stinted light
To which fate and film consigned him,
Who'd smile at his own lot
Even at one year old?

And yet his mother smiles.
Is it grown-up make-believe,
As when anyone takes your picture
Or some nobler, Roman virtue?
Vanity? Folly? The wiles
That some have up their sleeve?
A proud and flinty stricture
Against showing that things can hurt you,

Or a dark, Medean smile?
I'd be the last to know.
A speechless child of one
Could better construe the omens,
Unriddle our gifts for guile.
There's no sign from my son.
But it needs no Greeks or Romans
To foresee the ice and snow.

PERIPETEIA

Of course, the familiar rustling of programs,
My hair mussed from behind by a grand gesture
Of mink. A little craning about to see
If anyone I know is in the audience,
And, as the house fills up,
A mild relief that no one there knows me.
A certain amount of getting up and down
From my aisle seat to let the others in.
Then my eyes wander briefly over the cast,
Management, stand-ins, make-up men, designers,
Perfume and liquor ads, and rise prayerlike
To the false heaven of rosetted lights,
The stucco lyres and emblems of high art
That promise, with crude Broadway honesty,
Something less than perfection:
Two bulbs are missing and Apollo's bored.

And then the cool, drawn-out anticipation,
Not of the play itself, but the false dusk
And equally false night when the houselights
Obey some planetary rheostat
And bring a stillness on. It is that stillness
I wait for.
                    Before it comes,
Whether we like it or not, we are a crowd,
Foul-breathed, gum-chewing, fat with arrogance,
Passion, opinion, and appetite for blood.
But in that instant, which the mind protracts,
From dim to dark before the curtain rises,
Each of us is miraculously alone
In calm, invulnerable isolation,
Neither a neighbor nor a fellow but,
As at the beginning and end, a single soul,
With all the sweet and sour of loneliness.
I, as a connoisseur of loneliness,

Savor it richly, and set it down
In an endless umber landscape, a stubble field
Under a lilac, electric, storm-flushed sky,
Where, in companionship with worthless stones,
Mica-flecked, or at best some rusty quartz,
I stood in childhood, waiting for things to mend.
A useful discipline, perhaps. One that might lead
To solitary, self-denying work
That issues in something harmless, like a poem,
Governed by laws that stand for other laws,
Both of which aim, through kindred disciplines,
At the soul's knowledge and habiliment.
In any case, in a self-granted freedom,
The mind, lone regent of itself, prolongs
The dark and silence; mirrors itself, delights
In consciousness of consciousness, alone,
Sufficient, nimble, touched with a small grace.

Then, as it must at last, the curtain rises,
The play begins. Something by Shakespeare.
Framed in the arched proscenium, it seems
A dream, neither better nor worse
Than whatever I shall dream after I rise
With hat and coat, go home to bed, and dream.
If anything, more limited, more strict—
No one will fly or turn into a moose.
But acceptable, like a dream, because remote,
And there is, after all, a pretty girl.
Perhaps tonight she'll figure in the cast
I summon to my slumber and control
In vast arenas, limitless space, and time
That yield and sway in soft Einsteinian tides.
Who is she? Sylvia? Amelia Earhart?
Some creature that appears and disappears
From life, from reverie, a fugitive of dreams?
There on the stage, with awkward grace, the actors,
Beautifully costumed in Renaissance brocade,

Perform their duties, even as I must mine,
Though not, as I am, always free to smile.

Something is happening. Some consternation.
Are the knives out? Is someone's life in danger?
And can the magic cloak and book protect?
One has, of course, real confidence in Shakespeare.
And I relax in my plush seat, convinced
That prompt as dawn and genuine as a toothache
The dream will be accomplished, provisionally true
As anything else one cares to think about.
The players are aghast. Can it be the villain,
The outrageous drunks, plotting the coup d'état,
Are slyer than we thought? Or we more innocent?
Can it be that poems lie? As in a dream,
Leaving a stunned and gap-mouthed Ferdinand,
Father and faery pageant, she, even she,
Miraculous Miranda, steps from the stage,
Moves up the aisle to my seat, where she stops,
Smiles gently, seriously, and takes my hand
And leads me out of the theatre, into a night
As luminous as noon, more deeply real,
Simply because of her hand, than any dream
Shakespeare or I or anyone ever dreamed.

AFTER THE RAIN

for W. D. Snodgrass

The barbed-wire fences rust
As their cedar uprights blacken
After a night of rain.
Some early, innocent lust
Gets me outdoors to smell
The teasle, the pelted bracken,
The cold, mossed-over well,
Rank with its iron chain,

And takes me off for a stroll.
Wetness has taken over.
From drain and creeper twine
It's runnelled and trenched and edged
A pebbled serpentine
Secretly, as though pledged
To attain a difficult goal
And join some important river.

The air is a smear of ashes
With a cool taste of coins.
Stiff among misty washes,
The trees are as black as wicks,
Silent, detached and old.
A pallor undermines
Some damp and swollen sticks.
The woods are rich with mould.

How even and pure this light!
All things stand on their own,
Equal and shadowless,
In a world gone pale and neuter,
Yet riddled with fresh delight.
The heart of every stone
Conceals a toad, and the grass
Shines with a douse of pewter.

Somewhere a branch rustles
With the life of squirrels or birds,
Some life that is quick and right.
This queer, delicious bareness,
This plain, uniform light,
In which both elms and thistles,
Grass, boulders, even words,
Speak for a Spartan fairness,

Might, as I think it over,
Speak in a form of signs,
If only one could know
All of its hidden tricks,
Saying that I must go
With a cool taste of coins
To join some important river,
Some damp and swollen Styx.

Yet what puzzles me the most
Is my unwavering taste
For these dim, weathery ghosts,
And how, from the very first,
An early, innocent lust
Delighted in such wastes,
Sought with a reckless thirst
A light so pure and just.

APPLES FOR PAUL SUTTMAN

Chardin, Cézanne, they had their apples,
    As did Paris and Eve—
Sleek, buxom pippins with inverted nipples;
    And surely we believe

That Pluto has his own unsweet earth apples
    Blooming among the dead,
There in the thick of Radamanthine opals,
    Blake's hand, Bernini's head.

Ours are not golden overtures to trouble
    Or molds of fatal choice,
But like some fleshed epitome, the apple
    Entreats us to rejoice

In more than flavor, nourishment, or color,
    Or jack or calvados;
Nor are we rendered, through ingested dolor,
    Sinful or comatose.

It speaks to us quite otherwise, in supple
    Convexity and ply,
Smooth, modeled slopes, familiar rills. Crab apple,
    Winesap and Northern Spy

Tell us Hogarth's "Analysis of Beauty"
    Or architect's French Curve
Cannot proclaim what Aphrodite's putti
    Both celebrate and serve:

Those known hyperbolas, those rounds and
        gradients,
    Dingle and shadowed dip,
The commonwealth of joy, imagined radiance,
    Thoughts of that faultless lip.

The dearest curves in nature—the merest ripple,
 The cresting wave—release
All of our love, and find it in an apple,
 My Helen, your Elisse.

THE HUNT

for Zbigniew Herbert

I

A call, a call. Ringbolt clinks at dusk. Shadows wax. Sesame.
Here are earthworms, and the dry needles of pine. I am
hidden. Gems in their harness might be stars, picked out.
Lovely to see, trust me. And the stone is protection,wouldn't
you say? This is my stone, gentle as snow, trust me. Dark-
ness helps. Let us eat. The air, promise-crammed. And so
the poor dog had none. I saw three in sunlight. One had a
pearwood bow, like Cupid's upper lip. I whisper my love to
this rock. I have always loved it. Sesame. A caul, a caul.
Where is Lady Luck in the forest? Well, there's no moon.
Once I had apples. Let us pray. They have great weight,
the bronze fittings of Magyar kings. Their trumpets are
muted. But the tall trees gather here, friendly. What is that
fluttering, there? I can't make out. All the dark sweet dens
of the foxes are full of stink and safety. That was a tasty one.
Just to go down, there with pale roots and hidden waters.
O hidden. Is anyone hungry? He laughed, you know, and
shook my hand. I must not say that. O the dear stone. Owls
are out; mice, take warning. All those little squeaks must
be death-cries. You're welcome. Trust me, trust me. But
didn't he laugh? So help me.

I I

I am much too tired now to do anything
But look at the molding along the top of the wall.
Those orchid shadows and pearl highlights bring
My childhood back so oddly. They recall

Two weeks of scarlet fever, when I lay
Gazing at grooves and bevels, oyster whites
Clouding to ringdove feathers, gathering lights
Like snow on railings towards the middle of day.

Just to lie there and watch, astonished when
That subtle show gave way to electric light,
That's what I think of, lying here tonight.
Tonight the interrogations begin again.

EXILE

for Joseph Brodsky

Vacant parade grounds swept by the winter wind,
A pile of worn-out tires crowning a knoll,
The purplish clinkers near the cinder blocks
That support the steps of an abandoned church
Still moored to a telephone pole, this sullen place
Is *terra deserta*, Joseph, this is Egypt.

You have been here before, but long ago.
The first time you were sold by your own brothers
But had a gift for dreams that somehow saved you.
The second time was familiar but still harder.
You came with wife and child, the child not yours,
The wife, whom you adored, in a way not yours,
And all that you can recall, even in dreams,
Is the birth itself, and after that the journey,
Mixed with an obscure and confusing music,
Confused with a smell of hay and steaming dung.
Nothing is clear from then on, and what became
Of the woman and child eludes you altogether.

Look, though, at the blank, expressionless faces
Here in this photograph by Walker Evans.
These are the faces that everywhere surround you;
They have all the emptiness of gravel pits.
And look, here, at this heavy growth of weeds
Where the dishwater is poured from the kitchen
        window
And has been ever since the house was built.
And the chimney whispers its weak diphtheria,
The hydrangeas display their gritty pollen of soot.
This is Egypt, Joseph, the old school of the soul.
You will recognize the rank smell of a stable
And the soft patience in a donkey's eyes,
Telling you you are welcome and at home.

THE FEAST OF STEPHEN

The coltish horseplay of the locker room,
Moist with the steam of the tiled shower stalls,
With shameless blends of civet, musk and sweat,
Loud with the cap-gun snapping of wet towels
Under the steel-ribbed cages of bare bulbs,
In some such setting of thick basement pipes
And janitorial realities
Boys for the first time frankly eye each other,
Inspect each others' bodies at close range,
And what they see is not so much another
As a strange, possible version of themselves,
And all the sparring dance, adrenal life,
Tense, jubilant nimbleness, is but a vague,
Busy, unfocused ballet of self-love.

II

If the heart has its reasons, perhaps the body
Has its own lumbering sort of carnal spirit,
Felt in the tingling bruises of collision,
And known to captains as *esprit de corps*.
What is this brisk fraternity of timing,
Pivot and lobbing arc, or indirection,
Mens sana in men's sauna, in the flush
Of health and toilets, private and corporal glee,
These fleet caroms, *pliés* and genuflections
Before the salmon-leap, the leaping fountain
All sheathed in glistening light, flexed and alert?
From the vast echo-chamber of the gym,
Among the scumbled shouts and shrill of whistles,
The bounced basketball sound of a leather whip.

III

Think of those barren places where men gather
To act in the terrible name of rectitude,
Of acned shame, punk's pride, muscle or turf,
The bully's thin superiority.
Think of the *Sturm-Abteilungs Kommandant*
Who loves Beethoven and collects Degas,
Or the blond boys in jeans whose narrowed eyes
Are focussed by some hard and smothered lust,
Who lounge in a studied mimicry of ease,
Flick their live butts into the standing weeds,
And comb their hair in the mirror of cracked
      windows
Of an abandoned warehouse where they keep
In darkened readiness for their occasion
The rope, the chains, handcuffs and gasoline.

IV

Out in the rippled heat of a neighbor's field,
In the kilowatts of noon, they've got one cornered.
The bugs are jumping, and the burly youths
Strip to the waist for the hot work ahead.
They go to arm themselves at the dry-stone wall,
Having flung down their wet and salty garments
At the feet of a young man whose name is Saul.
He watches sharply these superbly tanned
Figures with a swimmer's chest and shoulders,
A miler's thighs, with their self-conscious grace,
And in between their sleek, converging bodies,
Brilliantly oiled and burnished by the sun,
He catches a brief glimpse of bloodied hair
And hears an unintelligible prayer.

THE ODDS

for Evan

Three new and matching loaves,
Each set upon a motionless swing seat,
Straight from some elemental stoves
And winter bakeries of unearthly wheat,
In diamonded, smooth pillowings of white
Have risen out of nothing overnight.

And all the woods for miles,
Stooped by these clean endowments of the north,
Flaunt the same candle-dripping styles
In poured combers of pumice and the froth
Of heady steins. Upon the railings lodge
The fat shapes of a nineteen-thirties Dodge.

Such perilous, toppling tides;
Such teeterings along uncertain perches.
A fragile cantilever hides
Even the chevrons of our veteran birches.
In this fierce hush there is a spell that heaves
Those huge arrested oceans in the eaves.

A sort of stagy show
Put on by a spoiled, eccentric millionaire.
Lacking the craft and choice that go
With weighed precision, meditated care,
Into a work of art, these are the spent,
Loose, aimless squanderings of the discontent.

Like the blind, headlong cells,
Crowding toward dreams of life, only to die
In dark fallopian canals,
Or that wild strew of bodies at My Lai.
Thick drifts, huddled embankments at our door
Pile up in this eleventh year of war.

Yet to these April snows,
This rashness, those incalculable odds,
The costly and cold-blooded shows
Of blind perversity or spendthrift gods
My son is born, and in his mother's eyes
Turns the whole war and winter into lies.

But voices underground
Demand, "Who died for him? Who gave him
place?"
I have no answer. Vaguely stunned,
I turn away and look at my wife's face.
Outside the simple miracle of this birth
The snowflakes lift and swivel to the earth

As in those crystal balls
With Christmas storms of manageable size,
A chalk precipitate that shawls
Antlers and roof and gifts beyond surmise,
A tiny settlement among those powers
That shape our world, but that are never ours.

APPREHENSIONS

A grave and secret malady of my brother's,
The stock exchange, various grown-up shames,
The white emergency of hospitals,
Inquiries from the press, such *coups de théâtre*
Upon a stage from which I was excluded
Under the rubric of "benign neglect"
Had left me pretty much to my own devices
(My own stage was about seven years old)
Except for a Teutonic governess
Replete with the curious thumb-print of her race,
That special relish for inflicted pain.
Some of this she could vaguely satisfy
In the pages of the *Journal-American*
Which featured stories with lurid photographs—
A child chained tightly to a radiator
In an abandoned house; the instruments
With which some man tortured his fiancée,
A headless body recently unearthed
On the links of an exclusive country club—
That fleshed out terribly what loyal readers
Hankered for daily in the name of news.
(It in no way resembled the *New York Times*,
My parents' paper, thin on photographs.)
Its world, some half-lit world, some demi-monde,
I knew of only through Fräulein's addiction
To news that was largely terminal and obscene,
Winding its way between the ads for nightclubs
With girls wearing top hats, black tie, wing collar,
But without shirts, their naked breasts exposed;
And liquids that removed unsightly hair,
Treatments for corns, trusses and belts and braces.
She chain-smoked Camels as she scanned the pages,
Whereas my mother's brand was Chesterfield.

My primary education was composed
Of daily lessons in placating her
With acts of shameless, mute docility.
At seven I knew that I was not her equal,
If I knew nothing else. And I knew little,
But suspected a great deal—domestic quarrels,
Not altogether muffled, must have meant something.
"The market" of our home was the stock market,
Without visible fruit, without produce,
Except perhaps for the strange vendors of apples
Who filled our city streets. And all those girls—
The ones with naked breasts—there was some secret,
Deep as my brother's illness, behind their smiles.
They knew something I didn't; they taunted me.
I moved in a cloudy world of inference
Where the most solid object was a toy
Rake that my governess had used to beat me.

My own devices came to silence and cunning
In my unwilling exile, while attempting
To put two and two together, at which I failed.
The world seemed made of violent oppositions:
The Bull and Bear of Wall Street, Mother and Father,
Criminals and their victims, Venus and Mars,
The cold, portending graphics of the stars.
I spent my time in what these days my son
At three years old calls "grabbling around,"
For which Roget might possibly supply
"Purposeful idling, staying out of the way,"
Or, in the military phrase, "gold-bricking,"
A serious occupation, for which I was gifted
One Christmas with an all but magic treasure:
The Book of Knowledge, complete in twenty volumes.
I was its refugee, it was my Forest
Stocked with demure princesses, tameable dragons,
And sway-backed cottages, weighted with snow,
And waiting in an Arthur Rackham mist

For the high, secret advent of Santa Claus.
Dim populations of elfdom, and what's more,
Pictures of laborers in derby hats
And shirtsleeves, Thomas Alva Edison,
Who seemed to resemble Harding, who, in turn,
Resembled a kindly courtier, tactfully whispering
In the ear of Isabella, Queen of Spain—
Probably bearing on financial matters,
Selling the family jewels for Columbus,
Or whether the world is round. Serious topics
To which I would give due consideration.
There were puzzles and, magnificently, their answers;
Lively depictions of the Trojan War;
And Mrs. Siddons as The Tragic Muse.
Methods of calculating the height of trees,
Maps of the earth and heavens, buccaneer
Ventures for buried gold, and poetry:
Whittier, Longfellow, and "Home, Sweet Home."
Here was God's plenty, as Dryden said of Chaucer.

Inestimable, priceless as that gift was,
I was given yet another—more peculiar,
Rare, unexpected, harder to assess,
An experience that W. H. Auden
Designates as "The Vision of Dame Kind,"
Remarking that "the objects of this vision
May be inorganic—mountains, rivers, seas,—
Or organic—trees and beasts—but they're non-human,
Though human artifacts may be included."

We were living at this time in New York City
On the sixth floor of an apartment house
On Lexington, which still had streetcar tracks.
It was an afternoon in the late summer;
The windows open; wrought-iron window guards
Meant to keep pets and children from falling out.
I, at the window, studiously watching

A marvelous transformation of the sky;
A storm was coming up by dark gradations.
But what was curious about this was
That as the sky seemed to be taking on
An ashy blankness, behind which there lay
Tonalities of lilac and dusty rose
Tarnishing now to something more than dusk,
Crepuscular and funerary greys,
The streets became more luminous, the world
Glinted and shone with an uncanny freshness.
The brickwork of the house across the street
(A grim, run-down Victorian chateau)
Became distinct and legible; the air,
Full of excited imminence, stood still.
The streetcar tracks gleamed like the path of snails.
And all of this made me superbly happy,
But most of all a yellow Checker Cab
Parked at the corner. Something in the light
Was making this the yellowest thing on earth.
It was as if Adam, having completed
Naming the animals, had started in
On colors, and had found his primary pigment
Here, in a taxi cab, on Eighty-ninth street.
It was the absolute, parental yellow.
Trash littered the gutter, the chipped paint
Of the lamppost still was chipped, but everything
Seemed meant to be as it was, seemed so designed,
As if the world had just then been created,
Not as a garden, but a rather soiled,
Loud, urban intersection, by God's will.
And then a chart of the Mississippi River,
With all her tributaries, flashed in the sky.
Thunder, beginning softly and far away,
Rolled down our avenue towards an explosion
That started with the sound of ripping cloth
And ended with a crash that made all crashes
Feeble, inadequate preliminaries.

And it began to rain. Someone or other
Called me away from there, and closed the window.

Reverberations (from the Latin, *verber*,
Meaning a whip or lash) rang down the alley
Of Lower Manhattan where George Washington
Stood in the cold, eying the ticker-tape,
Its latest bulletins getting worse and worse,
A ticking code of terminal messages.
The family jewels were gone. What had Columbus
(Who looked so noble in The Book of Knowledge)
Found for himself? Leg-irons. The Jersey flats.
More bodies than the *Journal-American*
Could well keep count of, most of them Indians.
And then one day there was discovered missing
My brother's bottle of phenobarbitol—
And, as it later turned out, a razor blade.
How late in coming were all the revelations.
How dark and Cabbalistic the mysteries.
Messages all in cipher, enthymemes
Grossly suggestive, keeping their own counsel,
Vivid and unintelligible dreams.
A heartless regimen of exercises
Performed upon a sort of doorway gym
Was meant to strengthen my brother's hand and arm,
As hours with a stereopticon
His eyesight. But the doctor's tactful whispers
Were sibilant, Sibylline, inaudible.
There were, at last, when he returned to us,
My father's bandaged wrists. All the elisions
Cried loudly in a tongue I didn't know.
Finally, in the flat, declarative sentence
Of the encephalograph, the news was in:
In shocking lines the instrument described
My brother's malady as what the French,
Simply and full of awe, call *"le grand mal,"*
The Great Disease, Caesar's and Dostoievski's.

All of this seemed to prove, in a world where proof
Was often stinting, and the clues ominous,
That the *Journal-American* after all was right:
That sex was somehow wedded to disaster,
Pleasure and pain were necessary twins,
And that The Book of Knowledge and my vision
(Or whatever it was) were to be put away
With childish things, as, in the end, the world
As well as holy text insist upon.

    Just when it was that Fräulein disappeared
I don't recall. We continued to meet each other
By secret assignations in my dreams
In which, by stages, our relationship
Grew into international proportions
As the ghettos of Europe emptied, the box cars
Rolled toward enclosures terminal and obscene,
The ovens blazed away like Pittsburgh steel mills,
Chain-smoking through the night, and no one spoke.
We two would meet in a darkened living room
Between the lines of advancing allied troops
In the Wagnerian twilight of the *Reich*.
She would be seated by a table, reading
Under a lamp-shade of the finest parchment.
She would look up and say, "I always knew
That you would come to me, that you'd come home."
I would read over her shoulder, "*In der Heimat,
Im Heimatland, da gibts ein Wiedersehen.*"
An old song of comparative innocence,
Until one learns to read between the lines.

THE GHOST IN THE MARTINI

Over the rim of the glass
Containing a good martini with a twist
I eye her bosom and consider a pass,
Certain we'd not be missed

In the general hubbub.
Her lips, which I forgot to say, are superb,
Never stop babbling once (Aye, there's the rub)
But who would want to curb

Such delicious, artful flattery?
It seems she adores my work, the distinguished
grey
Of my hair. I muse on the salt and battery
Of the sexual clinch, and say

Something terse and gruff
About the marked disparity in our ages.
She looks like twenty-three, though eager enough.
As for the famous wages

Of sin, she can't have attained
Even to union scale, though you never can tell.
Her waist is slender and suggestively chained,
And things are going well.

The martini does its job,
God bless it, seeping down to the dark old id.
("Is there no cradle, Sir, you would not rob?")
Says ego, but the lid

Is off. The word is Strike
While the iron's hot.) And now, ingenuous and
gay,
She is asking me about what I was like
At twenty. (Twenty, eh?)

You wouldn't have liked me then,
I answer, looking carefully into her eyes.
I was shy, withdrawn, awkward, one of those men
That girls seemed to despise,

Moody and self-obsessed,
Unhappy, defiant, with guilty dreams galore,
Full of ill-natured pride, an unconfessed
Snob and a thorough bore.

Her smile is meant to convey
How changed or modest I am, I can't tell which,
When I suddenly hear someone close to me say,
"You lousy son-of-a-bitch!"

A young man's voice, by the sound,
Coming, it seems, from the twist in the martini.
"You arrogant, elderly letch, you broken-down
Brother of Apeneck Sweeney!

Thought I was buried for good
Under six thick feet of mindless self-regard?
Dance on my grave, would you, you galliard stud,
Silenus in leotard?

Well, summon me you did,
And I come unwillingly, like Samuel's ghost.
'*All things shall be revealed that have been hid.*'
There's something for you to toast!

You only got where you are
By standing upon my ectoplasmic shoulders,
And wherever that is may not be so high or far
In the eyes of some beholders.

Take, for example, me.
I have sat alone in the dark, accomplishing little,
And worth no more to myself, in pride and fee,
Than a cup of luke-warm spittle.

But honest about it, withal. . ."
("Withal," forsooth!) "Please not to interrupt.
And the lovelies went by, 'the long and the short
and the tall,'
Hankered for, but untupped.

Bloody monastic it was.
A neurotic mixture of self-denial and fear;
The verse halting, the cataleptic pause,
No sensible pain, no tear,

But an interior drip
As from an ulcer, where, in the humid deep
Center of myself, I would scratch and grip
The wet walls of the keep,

Or lie on my back and smell
From the corners the sharp, ammoniac, urine
stink.
'*No light, but rather darkness visible.*'
And plenty of time to think.

In that thick, fetid air
I talked to myself in giddy recitative:
'*I have been studying how I may compare
This prison where I live*

Unto the world. . .' I learned
Little, and was awarded no degrees.
Yet all that sunken hideousness earned
Your negligence and ease.

Nor was it wholly sick,
Having procured you a certain modest fame;
A devotion, rather, a grim device to stick
          To something I could not name."

Meanwhile, she babbles on
About men, or whatever, and the juniper juice
Shuts up at last, having sung, I trust, like a swan.
          Still given to self-abuse!

Better get out of here;
If he opens his trap again it could get much worse.
I touch her elbow, and, leaning toward her ear,
          Tell her to find her purse.

GOING THE ROUNDS:
A SORT OF LOVE POEM

I

Some people cannot endure
Looking down from the parapet atop the Empire State
Or the Statue of Liberty—they go limp, insecure,
The vertiginous height hums to their numbered bones
Some homily on Fate;
Neither virtue past nor vow to be good atones

To the queasy stomach, the quick,
Involuntary softening of the bowels.
"What goes up must come down," it hums: the
ultimate, sick
Joke of Fortuna. The spine, the world vibrates
With terse, ruthless avowals
From "The Life of More," "A Mirror For Magistrates."

And there are heights of spirit.
And one of these is love. From way up here,
I observe the puny view, without much merit,
Of all my days. High on the house are nailed
Banners of pride and fear.
And that small wood to the west, the girls I have failed.

It is, on the whole, rather glum:
The cyclone fence, the tar-stained railroad ties,
With, now and again, surprising the viewer, some
Garden of selflessness or effort. And, as I must,
I acknowledge on this high rise
The ancient metaphysical distrust.

But candor is not enough,
Nor is it enough to say that I don't deserve
Your gentle, dazzling love, or to be in love.
That goddess is remorseless, watching us rise
        In all our ignorant nerve,
And when we have reached the top, putting us wise.

        My dear, in spite of this,
And the moralized landscape down there below,
Neither of which might seem the ground for bliss,
Know that I love you, know that you are most dear
        To one who seeks to know
How, for your sake, to confront his pride and fear.

11

No sooner have the words got past my lips—
        (I exaggerate for effect)
But two months later you have packed your grips
And left. And left eye-shadow, Kotex, bra,
A blue silk slip-dress that I helped select,
        And Fortuna shouts, "Hurrah!

Who does that crazy bastard think he is?
        I'll fix his wagon!"
As indeed she has. Or, as Shakespeare puts it, " ' 'Tis
Brief, my lord.' 'As woman's love.' " He knew,
Though our arch-scholiast of the spirit's agon,
        Nothing, of course, of you.

And what am I to say? "Well, at least it will do
        For a poem."? From way down here,
The Guy in the Lake, I gaze at the distant blue
Beyond the surface, and twice as far away.
Deep in the mirror, I am reversed but clear.
        And what am I to say?

Sackville would smile. Well, let him smile. To say
        Nothing about those girls
I turned into wood, like Daphne. And every day
Cavendish mutters about his Cardinal, scorned
Son-of-a-butcher. More God damn moral pearls.
        Well, I had been warned.

Yet when I dream, it's more than of your hair,
        Your privates, voice, or face;
These deeps remind me we are still not square.
A fog thickens into cold smoke. Perhaps
You too will remember the terror of that place,
        The breakers' dead collapse,

The cry of the boy, pulled out by the undertow,
        Growing dimmer and more wild,
And how, the dark currents sucking from below,
When I was not your lover or you my wife,
Yourself exhausted and six months big with child,
        You saved my son's life.

GOLIARDIC SONG

In classical environs
  Deity misbehaves;
There nereids and sirens
  Bucket the whomping waves.
As tritons sound their conches
  With fat, distended cheeks,
Welded are buxom haunches
  To muscular physiques.

Out of that frothy pageant
  Venus Pandemos rose,
Great genetrix and regent
  Of human unrepose.
Not age nor custom cripples
  Her strenuous commands,
Imperative of nipples
  And tyrannous of glands.

We who have been her students,
  Matriculated clerks
In scholia of imprudence
  And vast, venereal Works,
Taken and passed our orals,
  Salute her classic poise:
Ur-Satirist of Morals
  And Mother of our Joys.

"GLADNESS OF THE BEST"

for Hays Rockwell

Let us get up early to the vineyards; let us
see if the vine flourish, whether the tender
grape appear, and the pomegranates bud forth:
there will I give thee my loves.

See, see upon a field of royal blue,
Scaling the steep escarpments of the sky
      With gold-leafed curlicue,
Sepals and plumula and filigree,
      This vast, untrellised vine
Of scroll- and fretwork, a Jesse's family tree
Or ivy whose thick clamberings entwine
Heaven and earth and the viewer's raddling eye.

This mealed and sprinkled glittering, this park
Of 'flowres delice' and Gobelin *millefleurs*
      Coiling upon the dark
In wild tourbillions, gerbs and golden falls
      Is a mere lace or grille
Before which Jesus works his miracles
Of love, feeding the poor, curing the ill,
Here in the Duc de Berry's *Très Riches Heures*;

And is itself the visible counterpart
Of fugal consort, branched polyphony,
      That dense, embroidered art
Of interleaved and deftly braided song
      In which each separate voice
Seems to discover where it should belong
Among its kind, and, fated by its choice,
Pursues a purpose at once fixed and free;

And every *cantus*, firm in its own pursuits,
Fluent and yet cast, as it were, in bronze,
      Exchanges brief salutes
And bows of courtesy at every turn
      With every neighboring friend,
Bends to oblige each one with quick concern
And join them at a predetermined end
Of cordial and confirming antiphons.

Such music in its turn becomes the trope
Or figure of that holy amity
      Which is our only hope,
Enjoined upon us from two mountain heights:
      On Tables of The Law
Given at Sinai, and the Nazarite's
Luminous sermon that reduced to awe
And silence a vast crowd near Galilee.

Who could have known this better than St. George,
The Poet, in whose work these things are woven
      Or wrought as at a forge
Of disappointed hopes, of triumphs won
      Through strains of sound and soul
In that small country church at Bemerton?
This was the man who styled his ghostly role,
"Domestic servant to the King of Heaven."

If then, as in the counterpoises of
Music, the laity may bless the priest
      In an exchange of love,
Riposta for *Proposta*, all we inherit
      Returned and newly named
In the established words, "and with thy spirit,"
Be it with such clear grace as his who claimed,
Of all God's mercies, he was less than least.

POEM UPON THE LISBON DISASTER

Or, An Inquiry Into The Adage, *"All Is For The Best."*

Woeful mankind, born to a woeful earth!
Feeble humanity, whole hosts from birth
Eternally, purposelessly distressed!
Those savants erred who claim, "All's for the best."
Approach and view this carnage, broken stone,
Rags, rubble, chips of shattered wood and bone,
Women and children pinioned under beams,
Crushed under stones, piled under severed limbs;
These hundred thousands whom the earth devours,
Cut down to bleed away their final hours.
In answer to the frail, half-uttered cry,
The smoking ashes, will you make reply,
"God, in His bounty, urged by a just cause,
Herein exhibits His eternal laws"?
Seeing these stacks of victims, will you state,
"Vengence is God's; they have deserved their fate"?
What crimes were done, what evils manifest,
By babes who died while feeding at the breast?
Did wiped-out Lisbon's sins so much outweigh
Paris and London's, who keep holiday?
Lisbon is gone, yet Paris drinks champagne.
O tranquil minds who contemplate the pain
And shipwreck of your brothers' battered forms,
And, housed in peace, debate the cause of storms,
When once you feel Fate's catalogue of woe,
Tears and humanity will start and show.
When earth gapes for me while I'm sound and
    whole
My cries will issue from the very soul.
Hemmed in by Fate's grotesque brutalities,
Wrath of the wicked, death-traps and disease,
Tried by the warring elements, we have borne
Suffering enough to sorrow and to mourn.
You claim it's pride, the first sin of the race,
That human beings, having fallen from grace,

66

Dream of evading Justice's decree
By means of Man's Perfectibility.
Go ask the Tagus river banks, go pry
Among the smouldering alleyways where lie
The slowly perishing, and inquire today
Whether it's simply pride that makes them pray,
"O heaven save me, heaven pity me."
"All's Good," you claim, "and all's Necessity."
Without this gulf, would the whole universe,
Still stained with Lisbon, be that much the worse?
And has the Great Creative Power no way
To teach us but by violence and decay?
Would you thus limit God? Or claim His powers
Do not extend to these concerns of ours?
I beg our Maker, humbly, from the heart,
That this brimstone catastrophe depart,
Spend its fierce heat in some far desert place.
God I respect; poor mortals I embrace.
When, scourged like this, men venture to complain,
It is not pride that speaks, it is felt pain.

      Would it console those sufferers galore,
Tormented natives of that desolate shore,
If someone said, "Drop dead with peace of mind;
Your homes were smashed for the good of human-
      kind;
And they shall be rebuilt by others' craft,
Who shall inhabit where once you lived and
      laughed.
The North shall profit by your vast demise,
And by astute investment realize
Your momentary loss and fatal pain
Conduced, through general laws, to ultimate gain.
To the far eye of God you are as base
As worms that dine and crawl upon your face"?
This were to heap some last, insulting stones
Of language on that monument of groans.

Do not presume to soothe such misery
With the fixed laws of calm necessity,
With The Great Chain of Being, hymned by Pope.
O dream of sages! O phantasmal hope!
That chain depends from God, Who is unchained;
By His beneficent will all is ordained;
He is unshackled, tractable, and just.
How comes He, then, to violate our trust?
There's the strange knot that needs to be untied!
Anguish cannot be cured by being denied.
All men, in fear of God, have sought the root
Of evil, whose mere existence you dispute.
If He, Whose hands all motions can contain,
Can launch a landslide with a hurricane
And split great oaks with lightning at a glance,
They harbor no regrets at the mischance;
But I, who live and feel in wracked dismay,
Yearn for His aid Who made me out of clay.

Children of the Almighty, born to grief,
Beseech their common Father for relief.
The potter is not questioned by the pot:
"Why is my substance dull, why frail my lot?"
It lacks capacity for speech and thought.
And yet this pot, fractured when newly wrought,
Was not, we know, provided with a heart
To wish for good or feel misfortune's smart.
"Our woe," you say, "is someone else's weal."
My body must supply the maggot's meal.
O the sweet solace of my heaped-up woes:
To be the nest of worms in my repose!
O bitter calculus of averaged grief
That adds to sorrow, offers no relief.
This is the impotent effort of the proud:
To posit joys that they are not allowed.

I'm but a small part of the Master Plan,
True, but all beings sentenced to life's span,
All sentient creatures, as the statute saith,

Must ache through life, and end, like me, in death.
The bloody-taloned vulture in his day
Devours with joy the dead meat of his prey,
And all seems well with him; but soon he must
Bow to the eagle's beak, and bite the dust.
Man wings the haughty eagle with a shot;
And when at length it comes Man's turn to rot
Upon a battlefield, he becomes the swill
On which the birds, triumphant, eat their fill.
Thus are all creatures brother unto brother,
The heirs of pain, the death of one another.
And you would cull, in such chaos as this,
From individual miseries, general bliss.
What bliss! Yet weak and troubled you declare,
"All's for the best," in accents of despair;
The universe refutes you, and your pulse
Inwardly knows the argument is false.

Men, beasts, and atoms, all is war and strife;
Here upon earth, be it granted, evil's rife,
Its origin beyond our powers to guess.
Could it proceed from God's high blessedness?
Or does Greek Typhon, Persian Ahriman
Condemn to woes the ground we tread upon?
I reject such brute embodiments of fear,
Those deities of a craven yesteryear.

But how conceive the Essence of all Good,
Source of all Joys and Love, pure Fatherhood,
Swamping His little ones in storms of ill?
How could we plumb the depth of such a Will?
From Flawless Love ills can have no descent;
Nor from elsewhere, since God's omnipotent;
Yet they exist. Such paradox has checked
And baffled the weak human intellect.
A God once came to assuage our suffering,
Visited earth, but didn't change a thing!
One sophist claims He couldn't; in reply
Another says He could but didn't try,

Yet, someday, shall—and while they ergotize
Earth splits apart and all of Lisbon dies,
And thirty cities are levelled and laid plane
From the Tagus to the southern tip of Spain.
    Either God chastens Man, instinct with sin,
Or else this Lord of Space and Suserain
Of Being, indifferent, tranquil, pitiless,
Drowns us in oecumenical distress.
Either crude matter, counter to God's laws,
Bears in itself its *necessary* flaws,
Or else God tests and troubles us that we
May pass these straits into eternity.
We cancel here our fleeting host of woes:
Death is their end, our good, and our repose.
But though we end the trials we have been given
Who can lay claim upon the joys of heaven?
    Whatever ground one takes is insecure:
There's nothing we may not fear, or know for sure.
Put to the rack, Nature is stubbornly mute,
And in men's language God will not dispute.
It behooves Him nothing to explain His ways,
Console the feeble, or instruct the wise.
Yet without God, a prey to trick and doubt,
Man grasps at broken reeds to help him out.
Leibnitz cannot explain what bonds coerce,
In this best-possible-ordered universe,
Mixtures of chaos ever to destroy
With thorns of pain our insubstantial joy;
Nor why both wicked men and innocent
Sustain alike a destined punishment.
How shall this best of orders come to be?
I am all ignorance, like a Ph.D.
    Plato declares that mankind once had wings,
And flesh invulnerable to mortal stings.
No grief, no death accomplished his dismay.
How fallen from that state is his today!
He cringes, suffers, dies, like all things born;

Wherever Nature rules, her subjects mourn.
A thin pastiche of nerves and ligaments
Can't rise above the warring elements;
This recipe of dust, bones, spirits and blood,
No sooner mixed, dissolves itself for good.
Those nerves respond especially to gloom,
Sorrow and dark, harbingers of the tomb.
There speaks the voice of Nature, and negates
Plato's and Epicurus' postulates.
Pierre Bayle knew more than both: I'll seek him
    out.
With scales in hand, under the flag of Doubt,
Rejecting all closed systems by sheer strength
Of mind and command of stature, Bayle at length
Has overthrown all systems, overthrown
Even those bleak constructions of his own;
Like that blind hero, powerful in his chains,
Self-immolated with the Philistines.
       What may the most exalted spirit do?
Nothing. The Book of Fate is closed to view.
Man, self-estranged, is enemy to man,
Knows not his origin, his place or plan,
Is a tormented atom, which at last
Must condescend to be the earth's repast;
Yes, but a thinking particle, whose eyes
Have measured the whole circuit of the skies.
We launch ourselves, like missiles, at the unknown,
Unknowing as we are, even of our own.
This theater-world of error, pride and stealth,
Is filled with invalids who discourse on health.
Seeking their good, men groan, complain and
    mourn,
Afraid of death, averse to being reborn.
Sometimes a glint of happiness appears
Among the shadows of this vale of tears,
But it takes wing, being itself a shade;
It is of loss and grief our lives are made.

The past is but a memory of despair,
The present ghastly if it points nowhere,
If the grave enfolds our spirit with our dust.
"Some day things will be well," there lies our
    trust.
"All's well today," is but the Seconal
Of the deluded; God alone knows all.
With humble sighs, resigned to pain, I raise
No shout or arrogant challenge to God's ways.
I struck a less lugubrious note when young;
Seductive pleasures rolled upon my tongue.
But styles change with the times; taught by old age,
Sharing the sickly human heritage,
In the soul's midnight, searching for one poor
    spark,
I've learned to suffer, silent, in the dark.
    A caliph once prayed in his last disease,
"I bring you, Lord, some curiosities
From our exotic regions here below:
Regrets and errors, ignorance and woe,
Unknown to the vast place where You exist."
He might have added *hope* to his grim list.

from the French of VOLTAIRE

FIFTH AVENUE PARADE

Vitrines of pearly gowns, bright porcelains,
Gilded dalmatics, the stone balconies
Of eminence, past all of these and past
The ghostly conquerors in swirls of bronze,
The children's pond, the Rospigliosi Cup,
Prinked with the glitter of day, the chrome batons
Of six high-stepping, slick drum-majorettes,
A local high school band in Robin's Egg Blue,
Envied by doormen, strippers, pianists,
Frogged with emblazonments, all smiles, advance
With victorious booms and fifings through a crowd
Flecked with balloons and flags and popsicles
Toward some weak, outnumbered, cowering North
That will lay down its arms at Eighty-sixth.

THE LULL

for Allen Tate

Through a loose camouflage
Of maples bowing gravely to everyone
In the neighborhood, and the soft, remote barrage
Of waterfalls or whispers, a stippled sun
  Staggers about our garden, high
On the clear morning wines of mid-July.

Caught on a lifting tide
Above a spill of doubloons that drift together
Through the lawn's shoals and shadows, branches
  ride
The sways of lime and gold, or dip and feather
  The millrace waterways to soar
Over a tiled and tessellated floor.

A casual, leafy sprawl
Of floated lights, of waverings, these are
Swags of mimosan gentleness, and all
  The quiet, bourgeois riches of Bonnard.
  Or were, until just now the air
Came to a sudden hush, and everywhere

Things harden to an etched
And iron immobility, as day
Fades from a scurry of color to cross-hatched,
  Sullen industrial tones of snapshot gray.
  Instinctively the mind withdraws
To airports, depots, the long, plotless pause

Between the acts of a play,
Those neuter, intermediary states
Of vacancy and tedium and delay
  When it must wait and wait, as now it waits
  For a Wagnerian storm to roll
Thunder along the street and drench the soul.

Meanwhile, the trustful eye,
Content to notice merely what is there,
Remarks the ghostly phosphors of the sky,
The cast of mercury vapor everywhere—
Some shadowless, unfocussed light
In which all things come into their own right,

Pebble and weed and leaf
Distinct, refreshed, and cleanly self-defined,
Rapt in a trance of stillness, in a brief
Mood of serenity, as if designed
To be here now, and manifest
The deep, unvexed composure of the blessed.

The seamed, impastoed bark,
The cool, imperial certainty of stone,
Antique leaf-lace, all these are bathed in a dark
Mushroom and mineral odor of their own,
Their inwardness made clear and sure
As voice and fingerprint and signature.

The rain, of course, will come
With grandstand flourishes and hullabaloo,
The silvered streets, flashbulb and kettledrum,
To douse and rouse the citizens, to strew
Its rhinestones randomly, piecemeal.
But for the moment the whole world is real.

ANTHONY HECHT

Anthony Hecht's first book of poems, A SUM-
MONING OF STONES, *appeared in 1954. He is
also the author of* THE HARD HOURS, *which
won the Pulitzer prize for poetry in 1968. He
is the translator (with Helen Bacon) of Aeschy-
lus'* SEVEN AGAINST THEBES *in 1973, and
co-editor (with John Hollander) in 1967 of a
volume of light verse,* JIGGERY-POKERY. *He
has taught at Kenyon, Bard, The State Uni-
versity of Iowa, and New York University.
He has been a visiting professor at Harvard,
and is presently the John H. Deane Professor
of Poetry & Rhetoric at the University of
Rochester.*